LOVE IN THE AGE OF LONELINESS

Love in the Age *of* Loneliness

poems by

Bill Pendergraft

Copyright © 2024 by William Franklin Pendergraft
Edited by Elisabeth Blair

No part of this book may be reproduced or transmitted in any form or by any means, electronic or mechanical without the permission of the author.

This is a work of fiction. Names, characters, businesses, places, events and incidents are either the products of the author's imagination or used in a fictitious manner. Any resemblance to actual persons, living or dead, or actual events is purely coincidental.

Thank you to the Cold Lake Review, Contemporary Haibun Online, The Dead Mule School of Southern Literature, I am not a Silent Poet, The Lowcountry, Maya's Micros, PoemTown Randolph, VT, Safe to Chew, and Vermont Almanac, in which some of these poems have appeared.

Thank you to Sharon Lopez Mooney and friends at the Burlington Writers Workshop for their kindness.

Cover photograph of my daughter Emily.

First Edition
Library of Congress Control Number: 2024913011
ISBN: 979-8-218-46044-0

*For my wife, Jeanne Phillips
and my children, Emily and Will Pendergraft*

Contents

Preface 1

Migration 5
The Path 6
The Black Dog 7
Available Light 8
This Pleasant Lea 9
Stick Season 10
Saint Matthews 11
Learning to Swim 12
Paddling to the Stream 13
Poem for Joel Jackson 14
Phoebe 15
A Portion of the People 16
Old Man on the Beach 17
Letters from Truk 18
Parris Island 20
Manhattan Island 22
Pretending 23
Each Day Yawns Open 25
Lost Marbles 26
Hot Water 27
Recycling 28
Charivari 29
A Little Love for the Working Man 30
The Last Party of the Faculties 31
Washington Tryptic 32
The Young Immigrant Sanding Sheetrock 34
Mayo Clinic 35
The Shoes of the Fisherman's Wife 36
The Rock House Fire 37

Vision   39
The Memory of Existence   40
The Long Trail   41
The Eremocene   42
Mourning Dove   43
Insomnia   44
The Chicago Odyssey   45
The Big River at the Big Bend   46
The Beloved   47
Saving Dolphin   48
Rules of Survival   50
Robert   51
Rachael   52
Not All Men Are Golden Retrievers   53
May in Vermont   54
Nil Per Os   55
Come Clean   56
Mojito   57
Photograph   58
Love's Labors   60
Life Cycle   61
John and Samantha   62
Gelatin Silver   63
How to Help an Injured Bird   64
Garden Theater   66
Ford's Theater   68
Greek   69
Burlington Bomb Threats   70
Diet   71
Daughter   72
Conversations at the Lowcountry Boil   73
Lake Champlain   75
Choice at Menemsha Pond   76
Bosque del Apache   78

Lowcountry Estrus   79
Another Love Poem   80

HAIBUN   81
The Tooth Fairy   82
I've Got You Under My Skin   83
Life Flight   84
Lost and Found   85
Love by Memorial Mold   86
Morning Meditation   87
The Magic Hour   88
The Preacher   89

Preface
Love in the Age of Loneliness

Forty years ago, I founded Environmental Media to write and produce environmental education content for public television, departments of education, museums, conservation organizations, and not-for-profits worldwide. It was a time when we protected the environment, and many were hopeful that we could help heal a century of environmental destruction.

My travels led me on a continual worldwide tour of natural communities, and I worked with people who were dedicating their lives to conserve and protect wild places. During periods of reflection, I kept diaries of my observations, and the poems included here evolved from those stories. One person I met along the way was biologist and winner of two Pulitzer Prizes, Edward O. Wilson, who was teaching at Harvard and who introduced the Eremocene, an epoch he defined as human's material and existential isolation created by our destruction of life on earth. He described the Eremocene as our Age of Loneliness.

Many believe that we have just a few years to reverse our environmental course, yet we have entered an age where we seem to have lost our way in the woods, perhaps destined to turn over our governance to a self-enriching few, even as we celebrate our independence and freedom from tyrants. In the words of E.O. Wilson, "The real problem of humanity is that we have Paleolithic emotions, medieval institutions and godlike technology," describing the present as a terrifically dangerous time. The health of our democracy can only be measured by assessing the health of the planet—inventories of extinction, documentation of humans harmed by a degraded environment, an assessment of our general happiness. This collection of poems is called *Love in the Age of Loneliness* because of my belief that our human capacity for gratitude, empathy and love of living things may get us through a time of great complexity.

Bill Pendergraft
The Northeast Kingdom, Vermont

Migration

along the marsh
the body of the little clerk
below the reed
magnolia arms that stretched into the sea

I held him in my hand—a migrant warbler
eyes laid shut—a lolling tongue
no outward sign of harm
no broken wing or feathers gone
his feet curled like two fists

I have seen him once before
a young man back from war
who sat silently in class
his head down on his desk
he had crossed the gulf each season too
returning to his father's dock and nets
he did his work and like the tide
he was there and then he left

we never understood his loss or ours
no outward sign of harm
no broken wing or feathers gone
yet worn by long flights home
when no one took his life
he took his own

The Path
for Jeanne

today I trimmed the path you built
and set it right again

stones you carried in your arms
the edge you did not drift beyond

you raked the straw about
the bark of the exploded pine

and squatting on your haunches
made the footing firm

the ecosystem that you made
laid straight and true

is what I have of you
our company on the path we walked

those we brought
those who walked away

but most of all
the building of it

the planting of the stone
the harvest of the furrowed brow

our journey through the labyrinth
our partnership in soil

The Black Dog

the dog had always stood beside me nights like this
when wind swept the island down
picked among the shingles and mullions

tonight was different
different wind that grunted roots from graves
different dog
his tail held rigid like a snake

it was later
low wind around the myrtles and cordgrass
moon unspooled
ballet on the walls and ceiling

I opened the door and darkness rushed in and swallowed me
and the dog
nothing we could do
it lapped us up with its black tongue
we became the darkness too

Available Light

there are moments of light in the forest

they illuminate small coverts

and embrace us like willows

here we learn to use what we have

This Pleasant Lea

waves clatter on the beach
Edisto in fog across St. Helena
a fawn through the catspaw and myrtle thicket
and you
walking up the bank from Lucy Creek
joy in your sun-warmed arms

Stick Season

milky sky in late March
I lay a fire
another day through the mud
leafless forest
in three coats and stocking cap I head out
slipping your lists into pockets
warmed by your sympathy
cold-hungry-upside down
a tufted titmouse

Saint Matthews

cotton is in
clues on the roadsides
bales to the gin

all summer he had walked its seas
white froth of god and chemistry

the rolling remnant dunes
bowls in his palms like his firstborn girl

now rolled and sold
money in his pocket
all he thinks about is seed spent

Learning to Swim

drowning in your life
you rescued me
carried me to shore
gave me breath again
and looking up to see your face
I knew it was you
who pushed me in

Paddling to the Stream

far to sea
land drops below the curve
I am left only memories of marsh

stars remain
chaos of water
pelagic birds and fish

hunger to be among my oldest kin
I return to the recently living and dying

the way home

Poem for Joel Jackson

I found you today at The Bookmark
between Ginsberg and Lawrence
a domestic among imports

I scanned the foreword
you rest among the poets

last night I dropped one velvet paw onto Goat Island
light on the culling box
we kept shrimp and reds
tossed the rest

Phoebe

in this cold morning
she finishes
one fledged yesterday
the others today

she has borne insects from stoic searches
scaling maples and pines
to and from the nest as straight as sunlight

the product of it
kids who flew away
the quiet tangle in my eave
her own song

A Portion of the People

I sat beside him on the Battery
we were making a film about the Tribe

he told me he felt like an island among men and women
klieg lights and history

we both looked at the ballast cobble
weight carried until safely home from storm

he lighted a cigarette and we drove back to the Holiday Inn

a big blow came in that night and the lights went out
he spoke her name in sleep

next day we interviewed a man with numbers on his arm

we all walked out alive

Old Man on the Beach

waves of recollection
rolling up to his toes
as he stands in the wrack
expecting the sunrise

he wears his favorite shorts
she gave to him
one birthday one moment
long ago in some place
somewhere

he remembers to hold
in his stomach
as he thinks of her
the way she followed a false crawl
knowing it led to nothing

or ran her hands in his pockets
around him
thinking the things she thought
the daily forgiveness
the solemn kiss of constancy

and then it rose again
the illusion of fire from water
and for a moment
he was a believer
in just one more day

Letters from Truk
for Bill Lovin

1944

men
on porcelain seas
shared tea and cigarettes

polished brass shell
oiled their jeeps and tanks

in the shadows of the king posts
came the loading in
loading off
whirr of winches
ratcheting of coils of cable
cries beneath the decks
men of war
machines

moon
and light below from lamps
letters to those they loved
left

at anchor
stripped to the waist
leaning against the aft rail
smoking
staring across the reef toward home
they saw them come
whispering

you shall return
we shall fill you with the sea
beneath
below
beyond
your eyes and saucers will overflow with brine
guns of rot and rust
corridors of weed and sway
your letters
sediment

2004

I swim
hear my singing exhalations
down the listing sides of ships
between incisions of bomb and bayonet
resurrections of fans and polyps
your letters
in envelopes of pearl

Parris Island

every morning at dawn
the new Marines on Parris Island
stop dreaming of home
and belly-down for rifle training

Bin Ladin targets the squint and squeeze
the tattoo of small arms fire
as they hold their breaths
expecting an outcome

thinking of these children
platoons of boys and girls
across the bay opens up my chest
my heart balled with family photos in their duffels

from the halls of Montezuma
to the children who rode
the bus from home to Yemassee and
by the ruins of Sheldon Church

the floors are slick with their fear
blisters seep inside new boots
they are schooled in pain
they wake and sleep a walking wound yet

they find their fathers and mothers here
their lost brothers and sisters
their dreams of themselves to be
and they become the reality

they are weaponized

their arms soldiers of their minds
understanding is replaced with reflex
empathy with antipathy

where there was confusion
there comes precision
where there was calamity
there comes calm

Friday is graduation day
pink motels fill with cousins
fry houses swell with
young lovers and parents

who this day may imagine only this beachhead
the pledge of one American boy or girl
(west are the mountains at Caesar's Head
the sutras flown on flags the colors of the earth)

I have read about them coming home
surprised-dismembered by the fight
and as they've lost the will to give
some wish to take their own lives more

in the afternoon I'm left without them
in the dank dark marsh
the shooting stops the day is won
the staffs are planted firm

my grandchildren
sit beside me for a read
their small arms at my back
their fires ready for the stoking

Manhattan Island

in small groups of strangers
each holding a plastic glass of cheap wine
lip reading over the din
I think you said let's get the hell out of here
walk through the city to the sound
breathe the smog
watch cars fly south
go anyplace else

but that's not what you said
you said we must set up the booth by six
present in the ballroom at ten
sit with so-and-so at the luncheon
pack for the red-eye to the next one

when you sell yourself
make sure it's worth
young cabernets
cheese cubes
strangers
the death of the sea around us

Pretending

let's pretend there's a room
in a house built by the sea
the sea's perfume
from room to room
pretend you were here as a child
that you chose toys from chests
in the sunlit mornings
played alone among the pine planks
clattering up the stairs with trucks
and planes and shells
perhaps your mother led
you down the boardwalk
to the beach
where you visited the sea
that after the years you met your lover here
slept together in the small upstairs bedroom
that overlooks the forest and the sea beyond
turned the lamp out early
and laid together
telling lies and laughing
and perhaps you visit
old and alone again
as the rain begins
you walk through the house
a photograph of your father
home from war
a willowy child
climbing up the dune toward home
you have become the
light across the walls and doors

the bell buoy ringing
the foghorn as it sounds
at the inlet to the sea
and sea pours in
with bryozoans and fish
turtles and crabs
rising onto the beach
expanding like the universe
and just then you see
your son and daughter
walking down the beach toward you
they are old too
dressed in hats and scarves
they hold hands
they sit beside you
tell you that they love you
that all is fine
you're glad they're warmly dressed
perhaps not
maybe you sit alone on the beach
the tide returns
you are wet and cold
lifted by the sea
you lay back into the waves
and float far into the ocean
looking up as the sun fades
but you do not worry
after all
we are only pretending

Each Day Yawns Open

all day I fill the basket

a ripe tomato in my hand

warm green peppers in late sun

leeks pulled from black earth

the song of warblers home

children along the porch

careless-forgiven-almost forgotten

the wind licks up salt with sunfall

we taste it on our lips

sleep in fecund joy

Lost Marbles
for Stuart

he collected them for eighty years
steelies from his father
hiking with the other boys
bearings I always have them
drifting into the tangled wood
descending testicles in their hands

or from his mother the German sulfide
a small shepherd inside and those won
squatting on the playground
the crack of his shooter against another's
oxblood or cat's eye or in the sandhills
where the potters' kids shot with salt-fired clay

now standing in his fallow garden
smoking-wondering where they all were
like his penciled notes piled around the cottage
grocery lists—names of doctors
phones numbers of his children gone-forgotten

and later walking by the marsh in late sun
the tide over red devils-blue moons

Hot Water

waiting for voices from these hills
I walk where Palm Canyon Road peters out
into the land of the Agua Caliente
she counts money at the gate
issues three-buck tickets
her rattling silver bracelets
through power windows
into the infinite white land of leather and air conditioning

los fresas
their eyes to become satchels
wrinkled by men
sun
alcohol
miscreant children

the old white boys in silk golf jackets
learning to curse in Spanish
reaching out to their criado for a wedge
their hands slip into their coats
pressing against their skipping hearts
in allegiance to barbeque and alcohol

on the mesa
the people wait
a hundred years
a thousand
it shall be gone
like sand through your fist

Recycling

the grey mouse with soft white flanks
reclines on the wooden trap

like grandfather
laid this year on the dining room table

both were surprised
as they enjoyed an old camembert

we put grandfather in the barn until the ground thawed
buried him with the others when the serviceberry bloomed

the mouse
I laid on the fieldstone wall
turned into raven

Charivari

the second wedding lacks white
a peaceful compromise settles across your face like a veil

there is a high whisper in the corner
down the stairs
it clings to your legs like lint
a faint memory

you abandon yourself to this new man
his girth
his smells
his small movement when he sleeps
the way he holds his smokes

now
the fiesta
all heads back
mouths open to receive the kiss of joy
lost love leaving
rain of summer
grafts upon old roots
the bows of willows
compliant
stroking your shoulders as you walk

A Little Love for the Working Man
for Carl and Lilian Maria Anna Elizabeth Magdelene Steichen Sandburg

when he hammered metal roofing on the porch
the roof became a drum
a song in heavy storm accompanied our hearts
rain and coursing blood the river where we swam

a man who performed his work of tympany
who assembled orchestra of home and family
feet running down the steps from school and
she who danced her life away with him

we followed his music room to room and
in one great breath inhaled sound he shared
put our work away and seasoned stews for dinner
on the table he had made one warm summer

he had left his terrors for a time
to make the thing we gathered around
a useful man and the magic of his music
was its chorus growing larger with its singers

when they waltzed away they sang
as they left the meadow for the fir
into the deep the dark the lonely
when he all but disappeared with her

The Last Party of the Faculties

sleet tatters against the windows
the dark wood beyond the frozen lake

inside five house flies hatch in the warmth
of woodstove-candlelight-exhalations

all day they struggled against the glass
following light they believed was truth

then turn to the delicious party
drawn to all the red and flashing

their labella laid across crumbs of fruit cake
into pools of eggnog spilled upon the rug

two sit upon the Tiffany chandelier
abdomens plump and hairy but then

they fly from sugar and buzzing
one lights on the sticky beard of Dr. Whatshisname

another settles on a sweat of formula
curled under the Provost's baby's lip

five flies born in this false spring
the guillotined bud that opens in frost
the first flower that struggles through the freeze
you and I in failing light across the world
our arms tight around the other

Washington Tryptic

today we went to the parade
down Constitution from Seventh to Seventeenth
first men with flags then police on bikes and marching bands
Senators-Congresspersons-cute children on floats
twirlers of batons-dancers-horses
We the People with shovels

this morning four men on Connecticut
shoveling gray snow
they cut and cleaned
in parallel
from the shop fronts
to the curb
piling their frozen work
in great heaps
their exhalations
hot and white
their shoes dark with water
they are shovelers of snow
all that life sends down
scraped from the ground
pushed to the curb
rewarded by the breath

the lights from the rooms of insomniacs at the Hilton
rainbows of televisions abandoned
corners-eaves and crevices packed white
limbs of the leafless stinking sumac
cold black bones against streetlight
this little room on S street where I sit

I would invite you over for tea and biscuit
but you would become lost in this storm
and I fear freeze here

The Young Immigrant Sanding Sheetrock

a sweater wrapped around her head
my transport with her onyx eyes that said
do you think because you noticed
and wrote a poem
that anything is better

Mayo Clinic

arms around familiar waists
their stroll beneath
a canopy of galaxies
old friends who sit to go down steps

duet yet alone
without the other
doors that open
close upon themselves

with no shame
I watch the dance
this waltz of hope
that waltz of resolve

there are drugs
to dry those tears
religions too
but for now truth will do

The Shoes of the Fisherman's Wife

left on the steps
in white dunes of blowing sand
the slings erect and black
she hooks them as she passes
he is in the Stream
in lazy swells of fish
he licks salt from his lips
while on her porch
a cat curls down in the red afternoon

why do they come and go she asks
her breath white vapor in the bedroom
he turns to her in sleep
his flotsam frame surrounds her
she turns to the sea
the cat paws first light on the wall

she awakes to his phantom touch
knowing he is gone
and opening her eyes
blinks into the dark
she hears the trucks of fish
their engines whining between gears
and closing her eyes
a tsunami of cold

The Rock House Fire
Marfa, Texas

like love and hate
it began fast
wind blowing up from Mexico
spreading among the grasses
creosote bush and cottonwoods
firing up the high desert
fence posts telephone poles
junipers exploding in flame
black smoke and turkey vultures circling above
hot ash rising in the air
flying toward the Davis Mountains
onto the rocky mesas
smoldering out in blind canyons

cattle horses antelope pigs
ran before it
their eyes wide and wheeling
tongues bleat and slobber
blackening among the dry beds
smelling for water gone
escaping toward the highway
tangled in barbed wire
writhing and boiling in the flame
cooking on the stone and bramble
among news trucks from Austin

today it seems only a dream
overnight birth of grasses
weave among the prickly pears

ocotillo flash red
hummers cross the border
flying north toward nectar and the morning

Vision

in 1994 there was an earthquake in Los Angeles
and when the lights went out
Los Angelenos called 911
to report a frightening silvery cloud overhead
they had seen their galaxy for the first time

The Memory of Existence
for Raymond Carver

a couple at the car dealership
sit together in the showroom
waiting among windshield wipers and snow tires

he flips through a magazine
she looks for something lost in her purse

they call him and he holds her hands
explains he is leaving to pick up the car
he disappears through automatic doors

as she begins to weep
a coughing cry becomes a wail
others watch then stare at their phones
he returns and sits beside her
I thought you had left me she cries

tonight as I dance through our house
with the memory of your existence
I now understand what we talked about
when we talked about love

The Long Trail

we gather the language
calls of birds in the wood
songs of the wind and water
scrambles of mice in the maple litter
black bear stumbling toward us through the slash
our own heaving breath marching up Mansfield
we stuff songs in the pockets of our shirts
among soft petals stolen and
after all is said and done
the prayers and labors of it
the years wasted on remembering and forgetting
we sit to play for those we love:

this is my last song of the forest
my considered exhalations
my fingertips on the carotid
words sneezed and coughed into the world
around the universes and beyond
cells blown into the wind
comfort for hungry hearts
the last meal before the death itself

The Eremocene

as a child
grandfather paddled the salt marshes
called the marsh sparrows and wrens
who climbed the spartina to see

when he retired from machines
he flew home
marshes mitigated by interstates
spartina smothered in spoils
children following the money

when he cried I would rather be dead
his disjunct son flew in from the city
handed him an unloaded pistol
that grandfather placed in his mouth
pulling the trigger over and over again

we are to blame for loneliness
far from our natal shores
we encourage the colluding genes

Mourning Dove

who calls from the emergent pine
across the tidal slough
my hands and thumbs together respond
low lonely call of hope
and he calls back flies closer
here I am at the end of my time
and he alone searching for others of his kind
I call again and he responds
flies to the laurel thicket
carried by our chorus
so we both perch-call-wait
calling for comfort
calling for mate

in these times
we become both the caller and called
for if we no longer sing
what becomes of us all

Insomnia

last night I walked onto the porch
sat down in one of the rockers
watched the moon rise from the creek
and my dog followed
lay upon my toes
told me I had been a good friend
and I rubbed that place between his eyes

as the old moon rose above the trees
the shadows of the limbs
mapping the roots below
I pushed myself up from the chair
and returned to my bed

we looked so pleasant the dog by my side
both of us running in our dreams

The Chicago Odyssey

all day all night
the wagons roll down Huron to Northwestern Hospital
the siren songs invite each
one a broken heart
another gunned down child from Englewood
one who is drinking himself to death
a lonely mother jumped onto the L
each forlorn of us—sung onto the rocks

in the back the smells of sweat-piss and vomit
bandoliers of tape and gauze
swinging bags of seawater
whispers to strangers

tell him I love him
I am afraid
may I be forgiven

there is a Potters field in Lincoln Park
nameless thousands beneath a meadow
where children play
some smell of the great fire
others cholera
some war
most—work without reward

they come all day and night
the song is sad and sweet
the singing has no end

The Big River at the Big Bend

I came close to staying he thought
but wasn't the time
dodged a bullet.

At the Starlight Theater in Terlingua
he rises from the rusted chair
wind roaring down the arroyo
sand banking against the adobe
he shuffles home.

(Last time he visited Boston
she'd placed gardenias
in their wedding vase
pungent and brown when he left.)

With the supermoon
he remembered the grave by the Rio Grande at Johnson's Ranch.

Jack Holiday
Born 1912
Drowned 1933

The Beloved

night by the firefly surf
beneath the canopy of live oaks
tide receding
revelation of oyster reef

oh if I could stay forever
remain on the edge with you
right in the muddy moment

in passion
we conceive our future
in reflection
we flow beyond understanding

there is only this island
failing light
a croaking chorus
one friend

Saving Dolphin

today my dear I must write a feature on dolphin
just a few facts really
we have lived beside them all our lives
and more than once they've raced toward us
their sidelong thrusts pushing us apart
as they snatched a fish from the shoal behind
and became again the sea

I think they are blue
but at two hundred feet we are all blue
it is a blue world
confusing as the spectrum narrows
I have to remember where I am and who I am
and that someday I must return to the surface
dolphins remind me that we must rise to breath

and here is a female in the still shallow marsh of Lucy Creek
remember that day
we were in kayaks and watching with our paddles across the boats
she lifted her child to light and air
fed him her milk
lay still in the water together
terns and eagles flew over
the great blue lifted its head and squawked away

and out in the slosh and wakes
the pods of women and their children
and the big boys cruising the edges alone
water streaming down the smooth muscle of their backs
and flinging from fins and flukes in sunlight
boys and girls herding fry onto the muddy bank

gobbling them up like children at play
the fry jump and flash
driven upon the pluff mud

far to sea in the Stream they ride the bow waves of boats
fast and jumping from the sea
following fishermen snagging fish and shrimp from the nets
and turning over and spinning away in the froth behind the boat

and that dark hot night in the skiff before the storm slid in
when we rocked in Santa Elena Sound
our hands together—never seeing dolphin
but hearing their exhalations all around
the heaving gasps of desperate breath

and you will not forget the time we swam with them
downstream from Iquitos with the Ribereños
and the great pink gelatinous girls rode up by us
and looked at us through small dark eyes
their echoes ringing in our hearts and ears

but I need to write this feature on dolphin for the magazine
and today I ask a marine scientist
why they are all dying
and she said she doesn't know
but may before the money runs out

Rules of Survival

three minutes without air
three days without water
three weeks without food
one moment without hope

Robert

Robert who runs a little
crab boat out of Lucy creek
across St. Helena Sound
and who drops and retrieves
fifty traps a day, lives here too.
We sit on his dock, have a beer
and watch the sun set over Beaufort.
He says, "Hell, I've spent my life out there
winching up crabs and running them
to the fish house and even
set up a peeler operation
and sold live soft-shell for a buck each.
And look at me. My truck is rusted out
and busted, my wife died
and we couldn't afford a good
burial for her. Even now my boat leaks
and the engine needs an overhaul."
He raises his calloused cut hands
to the sky. The sea has worn us both.
We are storm-tossed, shot, spent,
hungering for touch each night.

Rachael

You moved to Raleigh from coastal North Carolina,
a secretary to the man.
He roused you with his passion for a policy document
written for the Legislature.

I watched you the day you lay down on Cabarrus Street
as the driver floored it through the light.
Perhaps you heard what I whispered
as I felt your thready pulse.

Not All Men Are Golden Retrievers

summer
diamondbacks rattling down the trail

slender wiry curly blond hair
and like most men didn't have a clue
imbued with a blanch of TV and Cheerios
earnestness that comes before disillusion
years before compassion

he had all the words—a bit of true meaning
yet disconnected from the informative wind
beaks and tongues that search the red canyon
things that teach dogs to hunker down and wait

but he looked into my old eyes
drove me to the coast
calmed himself by burying his fingers in my fur
watching me watch

I taught him
to sit
to stay
to speak

May in Vermont

peonies poke red heads through the clay
    lilacs last in the dooryard bloom

rhododendron leaves curl under in a late freeze
    red oak's hard cautious buds
confident apples fully leaf out
    red trillium scattered by the vernal pool

ramps die back in the hollows
    garlic a month away from scapes
bluets colonize the meadow
    trout lily and coltsfoot explode

hummingbirds fly back a thousand miles for sex and war
    robins soldier through the grass
red bellies bang on the roof
    jays yell in the beech thicket

the vireo's constant song
    ladybugs in the windows
ants in the honey bowl
    mice in the cellar hole

Nil Per Os
for Mary Lib

milk of her mother
salt of his fingers
tears of the children
tastes that linger

yellow squash
red tomatoes
lemon meringues
sweet potatoes

dinner with her children
great and grand
a meal to celebrate their painful gain
their painful loss of everything

all she had prepared
all who consumed her hours
all she left behind
her care of us—her greatest power

and at the ending of the day
her last request—no more
and she pushed her plate away

Come Clean
The Museum of Everyday Life, Glover, Vermont

as storm preys over Macks Mountain
the All Nighter scatters ash
cremated forest across the maple floor

as our Union parts I live in perennial storm
filth from our smokestacks and obfuscations
yet like a hopeful child I turn my face to the sky
stick out my tongue as if I have learned nothing

there is progress
a hippy shower and cold plunge
Bette Midler sings for gay men at bathhouses
Fred Rogers and Officer Clemmons
bathe their white and black toesies in the same tub on TV

and in Glover—Theresa Peura's bathing algorithm for her four children
come clean every day

Mojito

my wife and I become anxious
but beneath lies forgiveness
that flies in fast and splashes down

as we watch the swans landing
at the ending of the day
curling their necks around the other

they are there now
as we walk hand in hand
down to the pond to listen

but just when they're wooing us
they lift to the south
where they will forget us
and perhaps enjoy a Mojito

Photograph

today I am cleaning the house
sand vacuumed and mopped from floors
inspecting spiderwebs in corners
cleaning windows toward the sea

out on the beach
the weekend beginning
a reef of life up and down
the old fat man on his back in the sand
his peony belly

the middle-aged women
in their snug black bathing suits
with little skirts
lie on their elbows talking about the children
smoking and sipping gin and tonics

there are pods of surfers
with tattoos that spell **DEATH** or
the names of constellations
zinc noses and bodies of dried jerky
they paddle here
they paddle there

there was a little girl
she slithered into the waves without fear
as her mother searched the tote bag
for the towel

I'm doing little things today

I washed all the glasses
removed those hard water stains
hand dried them and put them away

Love's Labors
for the poets

we are in space—turning like bees around color
gathering and returning to build
to and from our tasks as straight as sunlight

we do not bend or waiver
we do not know of this or that
we go straight to it
a memory our mother whispered
as we fell upon our sleep

we have harvested honey
we have smoked the bee
and in her lethargy stolen all she meant to keep

it is a dream
not of keepers or bees
but the milky sweetness of the work
the melt of honey on the tongue

Life Cycle

back walk-up apartment
upon folded refrigerator boxes
a view of the moon through the transom

it continued through back-alley trash cans
to the old Buick back seat
until things fell apart
and the warming sun rose

then I noticed you
the cycle of your words—chrysalis to butterfly
the hopeful unfolding
that I would come to love
and love again

our future spread out before us
fully imagined
right down to the curtains
clapboard on Main
names of the girls
obligations

you said we are not the same the next day
when anger turned to forgiveness
and forgiveness to pity
we pity because we take pity on ourselves
we continued to cure this

John and Samantha

He was from Massachusetts, and she thought
he was the ticket out of her southern mosquito hole,
a place where nice clothes snared on catspaw and makeup
ran in the heat.

But he was glad to have escaped New York, the cold,
the poisoned water, the immutable vain rats.
She wanted to move to Soho.

He wanted to sip bourbon out on the river in winter
and catch a fish that was edible.
He founded a business. She had his babies.

They sat together for oil portraits,
blamed their misery on each other.
It was like they had been switched at birth.

The children had trust funds and regret they could never truly fathom,
like other things passed down.

Gelatin Silver

in the darkroom
he packs again his dreams that left only photographs

a thousand labels
wolves in Yellowstone
last year with the kids
the rumpled bed
tight shot—her lips

near the end silver strayed
gelatin of bones lost its attraction

he wants his arms around her
new babies sliding on the tips of his fingers
things he can put his hands on
he wants the details
their devils

How to Help an Injured Bird
from the New York Times Writer, Jamie Lowe, after Hurricane Matthew

        any bird that's lying sideways on the ground

prod their legs

        if they move there's a chance for revival

keep the bird warm
put it in your pocket
just wash your hands

        when birds go into a quiet dark spot they rest
        a brown paper bag is the perfect bird ambulance

wait until it becomes alert
let it go
don't throw the bird

        there is a fifty percent chance you may

save the bird

        ninety to two-hundred thousand birds die each year

from window strikes

        in New York City
        an ancient migratory flyway
        we are a real obstacle course for birds
        one third of all migratory bird species are at risk of

extinction

In 1970, New York Governor Rockefeller signed a bill selecting the eastern bluebird (Sialia sialis) as the state bird, the last state to select a state bird.

Garden Theater

it began in darkness
the rapture of rock
squeaking open rusty gates

before the sun
torpid heaps of harvester ants
upon the night's cold earth

mule deer browsing
javelinas scurrying up the wash
humans wrapped in damp sheets

some came singly in masks
long lashes red cheeks
others unclothed at first light

as the sun rose beyond Cathedral
building cairns of loss and hopelessness
signals of what had been what may be

they wandered forth
amid geology
past serpents and centuries
the dead beneath their floors

some equines
in heavy shoes
kicking the dust
cheered by the chorus of wind
and the lonely congregation

a quiet grace
through Tempe unawares
back to nothing at all

Ford's Theater

Each day we exit.

You, a box in Penn Quarter.
I fly south above the rivers-become-sewers, forests spent.

Just before the Metro closes, we enter the stage again
with the scripts of our play:

Scene 1—unending need
Scene 2—eliminating complexity
Scene 3—staring across empty sheets
Scene 4—a bent penny found on Pennsylvania.

Our lines are monologues.
We become the antagonist's stand-in.
You quarrel with the managers,
I with their hunger that eats the planet.

Then the chorus of our worries;
our child's child could grow dark,
osteogenic sarcoma could T-bone our plans.

Our deaf dog feels sound,
barks at everyone who walks by.

Greek

When my children talk about death
they say they glimpsed him
as if death walked by them on the campo talking on his iPhone
noticed but unknown
they use the word trajectory to describe their futures
their paths are ascending

mine is descending
not like the flaming arc of a falling star
but rather like something that has done all it can do
loses its gyre and coasts
they believe in vision
all I have is hindsight

I see death every day and sometimes mistake him for regret
but he is not regret
regret dresses in all those sad browns and a stuffy shawl
regret has sinusitis even on holiday in Tuscany

death means only that you have run out of Abate pears
and the hard cheese that you shared with the children
during the hike that summer south of Siena
when they walked just behind
sometimes placing their fingers on your shoulders
as they stumbled downhill from the ruins

Burlington Bomb Threats

I receive bomb threats
the metaverse erupts
the phone rings but there is no answer
like the silent shroud
that wraps Church Street in winter

I evacuate
shout warnings
but it's no bomb
it's the quiet death of fact

Diet

the solutions we humans have found

additions of those like ourselves

subtractions of those who are not

multiplications of our own seed

divisions by what we possess

our solutions are always ourselves
insoluble as husks

Daughter
for Emily

some may make a child
it is not simple and

like other things the whole is often
greater than the parts

for example—you can introduce
wood and string and pull just right

and make a song or at least sounds
that sound like song to some

or joining hands and turning 'round
two can make a dance

the idea of you first appeared
just like that and from promises kept

a knot tied here and there
we just held our breaths

and counted one two three and
you became the hope we had

but more than wood and string
and hands joined fast

much more than song
much more than dance

Conversations at the Lowcountry Boil

is that all—she asked
watching the sun set
over one-hundred thousand acres of spartina
stretching to the horizon

the dog is alert
to a twig falling on the roof
ignores hurricanes

my friends are depressed
from Thanksgiving to the new year
a most fertile time for fictions

each morning she feigns illness
so her partner can practice caring for her in old age
this morning she is paralyzed
and he puts on her underwear and socks
this is how they make love

they collect around oysters
fire and football
venison chili and hot wings
I chat up the poet
alone in the foyer

when she returns
for the holidays
I become thirty again
wiping peas from her chin.
and she becomes thirteen
hoping I will leave her alone

or die painfully
I hate these dogs she says
as she freshens their water bowls
and brings them bones from the butcher

the penny candy store beyond the El
where I first fell in love with Ferlinghetti
later in Chapel Hill
he read at Memorial Hall
we wept during the applause

Lake Champlain

Lake Champlain was an ocean
glacier gouged
salt water and whales
I said to my daughter
as we licked Creemees
watched children play on the rocks

I am no longer an ocean either
lonely for the human sea
milk running down my arm
reciting facts I still recall

Choice at Menemsha Pond

the fish
came down the bar
by the jetty
around the spit
to me

my line was in the water
active
as I have placed it there
passive
as having placed
I only wait

(the dark rain
that pelts my back
does not matter
nor what I've been
nor what I shall become)

nosing among the rocks
and frantic schools
that move as one
he idles
neutral in the
silo of the sea
barely notices
the tattoo of rain just above
the herding pelagics below

my bait
hangs between the two

and without thought
but not without reason
he accepts it into himself

Bosque del Apache

ephemeral as feathers
our small conversations
your day
tomorrow
children
a poem—Kooser—and then

lights out
your soles
pressed against my calves
like warm birds

from this slight nest
Sandhills by the thousands
blanket Bosque del Apache
to settle in the marsh

Lowcountry Estrus

at Santa Elena among the long lying
she placed cake on his tongue and laughed

he blushed or was it the July heat
here among the mosquitoes and epiphytes

wind among wave and pluff mud
boiling up through the rattling sables

marrying the nectar of gardenias
the sweat of pear and juniper

clothing cast over the limbs of angel oaks
island cotton shirts and blouses

flags of surrender
soaked through

Another Love Poem
For Ron Padgett

it is perfect

perfect for reaching wicks in all those hard to light places
invented by Baron Marcel Bich
who imagined his Bic in the hand of Miss Liberty
as he sat along Rue Jules Valles
admiring the perfection of his blue Bic multipurpose classic
that meets the hand like another hand in love

she didn't like Ohio Blue Tip matches
even if they said safety on the box
believing that they could be ignited by the restless claws of mice
we hear here and there in the walls
yet my blue Bic is ignored by mice
who may fear the flammable gas
perhaps can't reach the trigger
and the clever safety lock at the same time

my beloved
I will remember none of that
only the flames of our anniversaries
the fires we made beside ourselves
the votives I lit to remember you

HAIBUN

The Tooth Fairy

We carried her here in the rain. She was not afraid. She screwed her courage to the sticking place and looked into the intern's eyes, blue polyester scrubs, black snakes in his pockets. I don't know when we lost her. It may have been during Jeopardy or while her mother and I had tuna sandwiches downstairs. It may have been on the elevator or that moment I looked back to last week.

an arrhythmia—
just another winter night
took her teeth and all

I've Got You Under My Skin

The ash grew from a wind-tossed samara and she put down roots, reached for the stars. Abenaki took her offspring for baskets. Baseball needs bats, and the moody farmer wanted to get a handle on things, but she survived. She dodged an elderly cherry knocked against her in the '38 hurricane and patched over her wounds from squirrels and fire. But at one hundred, she lost her canopy as a little green larva bore in. It meant no harm. Why, we gnaw on the bones of calves we've named.

winter always comes—
the elderly die smiling
seed sprouting below

Life Flight
for Will

Flying late into the dark the life flight helicopter carries cocooned patients who frightened the exhausted resident who calls the sleeping attending. It wakes me as it flies over toward sick care, billing departments, and the possibility of creative imagination. Orderlies stomp out their smokes on the macadam, yawn in gowns and masks, cradle patients beneath the spinning blades and roll them through automatic doors, paperwork on their bellies like tags on loads of meat. I hear the blades accelerate toward home and I know I should go back to sleep yet concern smothers sleep. Was the hemodialysis enough, subdural bleeding stanched, baby cut from its pelvic trap, lung in cooler on time? They lift, now only craft and no longer cargo. I am trying to do better about sleep don't you think? I am trying to get ready.

lay me down to sleep
naked stretched upon the ground
on our mother's breast

Lost and Found

I walked the spring meadow to see if the columbine and red clover had survived the snow. Miles later, balanced on an ash log while crossing the beaver pond, I slipped and fell into deep mud. I lay there in the failing light and imagined myself in the minds of coyotes or perhaps a bear whose hunger might move him through the mud to me. I reached out for a buttonbush, pulled my feet from warm decay, and laughing at my foolishness stood to test how much was left. I was lost but knew where I had been. I reclined on a boulder a glacier left me twelve-thousand years ago and found my way again.

marsh meditation
on all that came before
remembering home

Love by Memorial Mold

Reading Emily Dickinson and facing again the brevity of existence, after a few days with my entire family, children, grandchildren and all. They think me dark, as it seems a family amusement that I bring a darkness to conversations, however my focus is on the insight that is brought to some by the continual awareness of our tentative hum. It is a joy for me to have that focus and to deeply appreciate the days, the simple acts of kindness and community. We are taught by contrasts and impermanence as birds are indeed taught by the snow.

the cicada chorus
their noisy reproduction
songs of the future

Morning Meditation

The phoebe pauses on the lilac limb, preening in the ceaseless rain. Above her in the nest she built herself, four hungry chicks plead. This morning a store clerk left her children with her mother and walked to work at Marty's 1st Stop. Midday she leans against the propped backdoor, breaking for a smoke.

young mothers in spring
pause in the rain
not thinking of things they must do

The Magic Hour

The sun is lying down across the White Mountains in a geologic dream about losing the coast of Africa and the big squeeze-up. I see it all happening at once, like the memory of an automobile accident, although this is no accident. Many events we earn degrees trying to understand are well beyond even our generational ken. And just when we think we know, someone finds a pebble and new galaxies are discovered.

glaciers are whimsy
a passing sneeze among stars
our life an eye blink

The Preacher

I lived alone in Vermont, among thousands of acres of forest in the Northeast Kingdom. I was unlikely to see another person, however deer and bear would amble through and there was the nightly call of the barred owl. One companion was always on the same beech branch, always singing: the red-eyed vireo. I could plainly hear him. Often called The Preacher, his song was clear, repetitive, and tireless like the ring of a summoning bell. Hearing his call, I thought of E.O. Wilson and our loss of natural diversity; my companions calling for me to pay attention.

summers in the beech
our natural companions
fewer voices heard

Bill Pendergraft founded Environmental Media to write and produce environmental education media for public and not-for-profit organizations worldwide. During his travels he met those working to protect and preserve the natural world and he kept extensive diaries of his reflections about people and place. His new book, *Love in the Age of Loneliness*, is a collection of poetry written during his travels. Bill lives in the Northeast Kingdom of Vermont.

For more information visit: www.environmentalmedia.com

www.ingramcontent.com/pod-product-compliance
Lightning Source LLC
LaVergne TN
LVHW041341080426
835512LV00006B/568